PARAMEDICS TO THE RESCUE

When Every Second Counts

by Michael Silverstone

Reading Consultant:
Timothy Rasinski, Ph.D.
Professor of Reading Education
Kent State University

Content Consultant:
Stephen J. Philipe, Sr.
Board of Governors
National Association of
Emergency Medical Technicians

Red Brick™ Learning

Published by Red Brick™ Learning
7825 Telegraph Road, Bloomington, Minnesota 55438
http://www.redbricklearning.com

Library of Congress Cataloging-in-Publication Data
Silverstone, Michael, 1958–
    Paramedics to the rescue: when every second counts / by Michael
    Silverstone; reading consultant Timothy Rasinski.
        p. cm.
    Includes bibliographical references and index.
    ISBN 0-7368-3849-X (soft cover)—ISBN 0-7368-3877-5 (hard cover)
    1. Allied health personnel—Juvenile literature. I. Title.
R697.A4S495 2004
610.69—dc22
                            2004003490

Created by Kent Publishing Services, Inc.
Designed by Signature Design Group, Inc.
Edited by Jerry Ruff, Managing Editor, Red Brick™ Learning
Red Brick™ Learning Editorial Director: Mary Lindeen

This publisher has made every effort to trace ownership of all copyrighted
material and to secure necessary permissions. In the event of any questions
arising as to the use of any material, the publisher, while expressing regret for
any inadvertent error, will be happy to make necessary corrections.

Photo Credits:
Page 9, Owen Franken, Corbis; pages 14, 16, 21, 23, Bettmann/Corbis; pages
24, 26, courtesy of the Miami-Dade Fire Rescue/Captain Al Cruz; page 29, John
Framar, Cordiay Photo Library/Corbis; page 31, Richard Ambo, Corbis/Sygma;
page 32, Wally McNamee, Corbis; pages 33 (top), 41, Pictimpact/Corbis; page
33 (bottom), Bob Krist/Corbis; page 34, Michael Kitchel, APWorldwide/The
Commercial Review; page 38, Index Stock Imagery; page 42, Chris Martinez, La
Opinion; page 48, 911 Pictures; page 53, Viviane Moos/Corbis; page 55, Greg
Smith, Corbis/SABA; page 59, Gabe Palmer/Corbis

Printed in the United States of America.

1 2 3 4 5 6 09 08 07 06 05 04

Table of Contents

*Two paramedics are ready as a dispatcher
answers a 9-1-1 call for help.*

CHAPTER 1

Emergency!

It is 10:30 P.M. on a cool night in April. Jen Sell and her fellow paramedics are sitting and talking in their fire station. Suddenly a call comes over their radio.

"Attention, Amherst paramedics. There is a two-car motor vehicle crash at the south corner of Elm Street and Pleasant Street—with injuries."

Quick Response

Lights flash atop the ambulance. Cars on the highway pull over to the right to let the ambulance pass. Inside the ambulance, two paramedics are calm and focused. Soon, the ambulance arrives at the accident scene. Police have stopped traffic so the paramedics can drive up to the two crashed cars.

---

dispatcher: a person who receives emergency calls and sends out emergency workers
emergency: an event that develops suddenly and calls for action right away
ambulance: a special vehicle for carrying injured or sick people
focus: to pay close attention to something

At the Scene

The police officers have put orange cones on the road near the two crashed cars. This helps them direct traffic around the accident. A fire truck stands by in case one of the cars catches fire.

Jen and her partner look at the cars. Both cars are crumpled—one on the driver's side, the other in front. One of the cars has white smoke coming from under the hood. The driver is still inside this car. He is sitting at the steering wheel. There is blood on his forehead.

As a paramedic, Jen has a series of jobs to do. She focuses on each one.

---

forehead: the part of the face above the eyes

A Paramedic's Checklist

BE SAFE

Observe and understand the dangers of the scene before moving in to help.

ARRIVE PREPARED

Have enough help and equipment to give first aid or advanced life support.

GET INFORMATION

Find out who is hurt and how badly.

STOP THE HARM

Give first aid, stop any bleeding, and give oxygen and comfort if needed.

GET GOING

Quickly get the injured ready to be transported to a hospital.

---

oxygen: the gas we need to breathe and live

BE SAFE

Before getting out of her vehicle, Jen looks the scene over carefully for any dangers to her and her partner. These dangers could include gasoline spills or downed electrical wires.

As she walks toward the first car, she remembers what she was taught:

It is important to know the dangers at a scene. Sometimes going into danger is a choice. It should always be a conscious choice. We must always be as safe as possible.

But Jen can see that the scene is safe. Firefighters and police have already secured the area. Jen knows she can move in to give medical assistance.

"Hello. I'm Jen," she says to the injured driver. "I'm with EMS. I'm here to help. Can you tell me where it hurts?"

---

conscious: thought about; considered
secure: to make free from danger
EMS: Emergency Medical Service

As Jen carefully listens to the injured man, she knows she is ready to help him. Before they even received the call, Jen and her partner made sure all the lifesaving equipment on their ambulance was working and in good supply. This means they had enough oxygen, bandages, medicine, other supplies, and tools to respond to a variety of emergencies.

Paramedics check the condition of an accident victim.

GET INFORMATION

Jen gathers as much information as she can about the injured person. She asks how he feels. She asks about his medical history. This information will help doctors at the hospital treat the injured person.

As Jen talks to the driver, she looks more closely at the blood on his forehead. She also suspects a neck injury. She doesn't want his neck or head to move. That might cause further damage. So she asks her partner for a cervical collar to place around the injured man's neck. She then carefully applies the collar.

Jen asks more questions. The man says he feels dizzy. He is alert and breathing well. She asks him if he can describe the accident. This checks the person's memory. Jen carefully watches him as he talks to see if his condition is stable.

---

cervical: relating to a neck
medical history: information about a person's past injuries, illnesses, and medicines taken
stable: staying the same; not getting worse

Jen applies bandages to the wound on the man's forehead. She then puts an oxygen mask over his mouth and nose to help him breathe.

Jen and her partner now remove the man from the car and strap him on a spine board. They do this to immobilize him and prevent further injury to his spine. Then they strap him to a stretcher and move him to the ambulance.

Jen continues to talk to the patient as he is loaded into the ambulance. She asks him more questions about how he feels. These questions provide more information about his health. But they also comfort the man. He knows that he is not alone and is being helped.

spine board: a hard, flat surface a person lies on that keeps the backbone from moving
immobilize: to keep from moving
stretcher: a light bed, sometimes on wheels, used to carry injured or sick people

Jen is not alone, either. She is part of a team of people who help in emergencies like this. Her job is to keep patients alive, to prevent further injury, and to take them safely to the hospital.

It takes about 25 minutes for the ambulance to drive to the hospital. Jen's partner again turns on the flashing lights and siren. Traffic pulls over to the right to let them pass by.

On the way, Jen sits next to the injured man. She uses her cell phone to tell the doctors they are coming. She also tells the doctors about the man's injuries. The doctors give her advice on treatment. Jen continues to talk to the man and monitor his health.

Finally, they arrive at the hospital. Jen and her partner bring the man into the emergency room. It is now time for the doctors and nurses to take over. It is also time for Jen to write a report about the accident.

---

treatment: a course of action
monitor: to closely watch

Paramedics bring an injured man to the emergency room.

How Did the Paramedics Begin?

Today, there are thousands of paramedics like Jen Sell in the United States and Canada. But not long ago, paramedics did not exist. So who do you think helped sick or injured people before they got to the hospital? In Chapter 2, you'll find out!

Before there were paramedics, police officers and firefighters assisted and transported people who were sick or injured.

The History of Paramedics

It's a spring day in New York in 1959. A woman is overcome by smoke in a burning building. An emergency dispatcher radios police and fire crews for help. These crews will need to transport this woman to a hospital before she can receive medical help.

Early Medical Help

Before the 1960s, there were no paramedics like Jen Sell in Chapter 1. Police, fire crews, and even undertakers transported sick and injured people to hospitals. These people did not have proper medical training. Many sick or injured people died because crucial care did not start until they got to a hospital. There needed to be a better way.

---

undertaker: a person who arranges funerals
crucial: the most important

A Better Way

The United States was not the only country trying to figure out a better way to give emergency care. In Russia, even before 1960, emergency crews began to include a doctor, a nurse, and a special assistant. In Germany, doctors began to ride along with ambulances as early as 1961. About the same time, doctors in Toulouse, France, did the same.

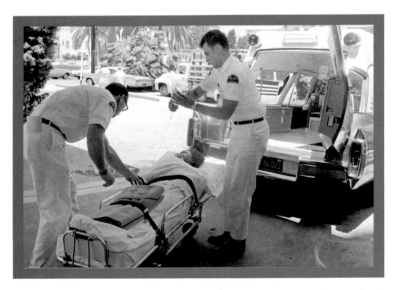

The 1960s marked the beginning of ambulances with medical staff aboard.

The Flying Squad

But the person who most influenced EMS in the United States was a doctor from Ireland named J. Frank Pantridge. Dr. Pantridge was head of the cardiology department at Royal Victoria Hospital in Belfast, Ireland. He had done research on heart attack victims and found that men who died from heart attacks often did so within one hour of the attack. To save them, doctors had to get to them more quickly.

In 1966, Dr. Pantridge put doctors on ambulance crews to treat victims of heart attacks. Pantridge's crew was so quick, they were nicknamed, "The Flying Squad."

Doctors in the United States liked this idea of a "doctor on wheels." Similar crews soon started in several U.S. cities. Getting doctors to sick and injured people faster saved many lives. But there was still a problem. Many U.S. cities were very large. There were not enough doctors to form enough crews to cover them. A new type of rescuer needed to be trained.

New Training

In 1967, the Miami fire department began to teach its firefighters medical skills. When these firefighters had to treat a sick or injured person, they got advice from doctors by two-way radio. They could then treat the patient at the scene, and on the way to the hospital.

The first ambulances looked like this and had very basic equipment. The paramedics spoke to doctors on radios for advice on how to help patients.

Medically trained firefighters began to save many lives. Others besides doctors could now give critical treatment at the scene of an emergency. These people became the first paramedics in the United States.

Lost Lives

As the United States became a nation of drivers, the need for prompt medical response grew. For example, in the mid-1960s, more than 50,000 people died in car crashes each year. There had to be a way to quickly get help to people and save lives.

First Steps

The U.S. federal government decided to create an Emergency Medical System. The government gave fire departments money for medical training, trucks, and tools. This meant that many more individuals could become paramedics.

Emergency care improved quickly. In 1971, the United States had only 12 paramedic units. By 1975, most of the country had paramedics who could reach injured people within a half hour.

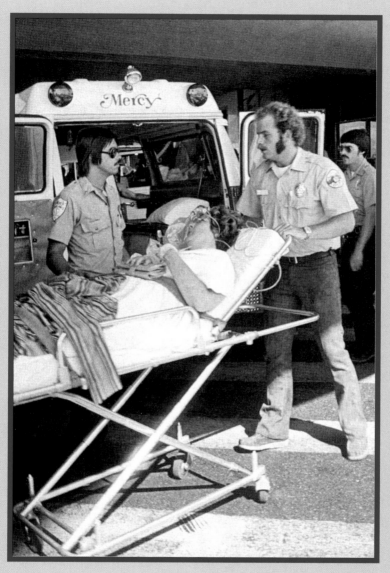

Paramedics at the scene of an accident in Nevada, 1977

The Good News Spreads

Despite the growth of paramedic units, many people still knew little about them. This would soon change, and TV would help change it.

From 1972 to 1977, a weekly TV show about paramedics aired. This popular action series was called "Emergency!" Soon, people nationwide were aware of paramedics and their work.

In 1974, the TV news show "60 Minutes" did a story about a new paramedic program in Seattle. The Seattle program was so successful, "60 Minutes" proclaimed Seattle "the best place in the world to have a heart attack."

Shows like these helped make the work of paramedics better known. They also showed how important pre-hospital emergency care is for all communities.

---

air: to show, tell, or broadcast
pre-hospital: before arriving at a hospital

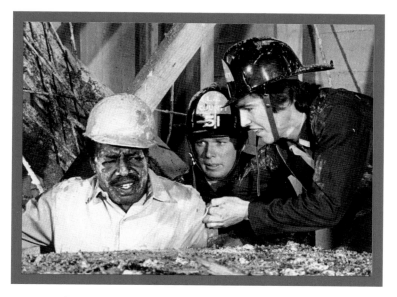

A scene from the 1970s TV Show, "Emergency!"

Times Change

Today, it is hard to believe that the idea of paramedics is still fairly new. Yet emergency care has come a long way since the 1960s. Paramedics now have the tools and the training to make daring, lifesaving rescues almost anywhere!

So what sort of daring rescues are paramedics called to make? What other kinds of emergency care do they provide? Read on to learn more about some amazing paramedic rescues.

Capt. Al Cruz (left) and Lt. Ernie Jillson (right) run a special program called Venom 1. This program helps save snakebite victims across the United States.

CHAPTER 3

Amazing Rescues

On September 12, 2001, a plane streaked across the sky on a desperate mission. A 62-year-old man had been bitten by a poisonous snake called a taipan. The plane carried a precious cargo—antivenin— to save the man's life!

Venom 1 to the Rescue!

Al Cruz and Ernie Jillson are firefighters and paramedics with the Miami-Dade Fire Rescue Department. They run a program for snakebite victims called Venom 1. Begun in 1998, Venom 1 has supplies of antivenin for most of the world's deadly snakes.

On September 11, 2001, Venom 1 got a call. A snakekeeper named Lawrence van Sertima had been bitten by a taipan as he was returning it to its cage. This snake is one of the deadliest in the world.

---

antivenin: medicine used to prevent poisoning from a snakebite
venom: the poison of some snakes, spiders, scorpions, and other animals

A Life-and-Death Search

Paramedics rushed van Sertima to the hospital, where doctors hooked him up to a ventilator to help him breathe. For 16 hours, they tried to save his life with doses of antivenin. But van Sertima remained deathly ill, and the antivenin was running out!

The Venom 1 team called hospitals and zoos all over the country. Finally, at 1:30 A.M., September 12, Cruz found more taipan antivenin. The San Diego Zoo had the only other supply in North America!

Capt. Cruz (left) and Lt. Scott Mullin

---

ventilator: a machine that allows air to pass through to a person's lungs

Flight for Life

Cruz needed to get the antivenin cross-country from San Diego to Miami. How? Since terrorists had used planes in a deadly attack in the United States a day earlier, all planes were grounded. But van Sertima needed the antivenin, or he might not live through the night.

Finally, Cruz convinced government authorities to allow an air ambulance to fly from San Diego to Miami. At the hospital, van Sertima was given extra doses of the antivenin. He lived.

"The reason I am here today is because of Al Cruz," van Sertima later said.

---

ground: to keep from flying

Rescue by Helicopter

In 1991, Coast Guard paramedic Dave Moore received a call. A sailboat had tipped over in a storm off the Massachusetts coast, spilling three sailors into the rough waters. When a Coast Guard vessel sent a raft with three rescuers to save them, the capsized sailboat crashed into and sank the raft. Now, there were three sailors and three rescuers struggling in the choppy waters.

Moore and his elite crew of rescue swimmers flew their helicopter to the scene. Called Aviation Survival Technicians, the crew was trained for such rescues. But the weather was worse than Moore had worked in before. Nonetheless, he jumped 15 feet from the helicopter into crushing 30-foot waves.

elite: thought to be the finest or best
aviation: the science, skill, or work of flying airplanes

The inside of a Coast Guard rescue helicopter with its medical supplies is similar to the inside of an ambulance.

Off Target

But Moore had jumped too far from the sailboat. High waves sent him farther and farther away.

"There were times when I lost sight of everybody. I couldn't even see the helicopter," Moore later said.

Moore was winched up into the helicopter for a second jump. This time, he landed closer. The crew then lowered a rescue basket into the water. One by one, the sailors and rescuers climbed into the basket and were lifted to the safety of the helicopter.

winch: to pull up something using a rope wrapped around a drum, which is turned by a crank or motor

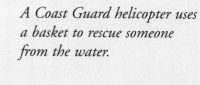

A Coast Guard helicopter uses a basket to rescue someone from the water.

More Amazing Rescues

Saving a person from a deadly snake bite and rescuing sailors at sea are only two of the many ways paramedics provide emergency medical care. Paramedics also work on special operations teams in the military, at industrial plants, with police SWAT teams, on life flights, and on high-angle rescues, to name just a few. The photographs on pages 32 and 33 show some other ways paramedics rescue people.

Paramedics help injured soldiers on battlefields.

Paramedics attend to injured workers at factories and plants.

Paramedics are part of mountain rescue teams that save injured hikers.

Now It's Your Turn

As you can see, being a paramedic takes knowledge, training, and skill. It also takes daring. The next chapter gives you a chance to use what you have learned or know about a paramedic's job in some common emergency situations.

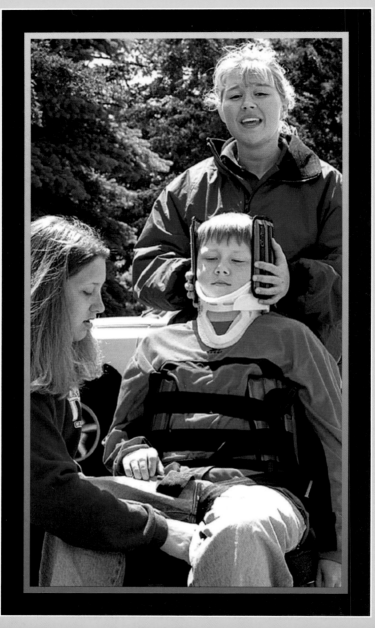

*High-school students being trained
to become First Responders*

CHAPTER 4

What Would You Do?

"How do paramedics know the right thing to do?"
asks Shameeka, a student on a field trip to her local
EMS headquarters.

"It's something you learn over time," the paramedic
answers. "But before any of us ever went out on an
emergency call, we went to school and watched
and learned by riding along and talking with
other paramedics."

"Boy, I wish I could do that!" Shameeka says.

Going for a Ride

How would you like to be a paramedic?
What would it be like? Do you think you
would be good at it?

Here is a chance for you to put yourself
in a paramedic's shoes. How would you
respond to emergencies like the ones that
follow, which paramedics may face on any
given day?

A Bad Fall

A call comes over the radio. A man has fallen off a ladder while painting his house. You and your partner jump into the ambulance and drive to the scene. When you arrive, the man's wife tells you what happened. Her husband is lying on the ground, next to the ladder. He is awake, but his back hurts.

As you talk to the man's wife, you can see she is very upset. She is sweating a lot and rubs her jaw as she speaks.

Your partner finds the man's back is bruised, but no bones seem to be broken. You apply a cervical collar to his neck and help put him on a spine board to take him to the ambulance.

Still, the emergency is not over. There is something else wrong here. Any idea what it is?

Who Is in Trouble?

The woman's sweating and jaw pain are some of the early signs of a possible heart attack. Luckily, you recognize the symptoms. You can give her the help she needs right away.

Signs of a Possible Heart Attack

- **Pressure or pain in the chest**
- **Difficulty breathing**
- **Sharp pain in the jaw or arm**
- **Heavy perspiration**

symptom: something that shows you have an illness or injury
perspiration: sweat

Bad Feeling

Another time, your team is called to a home. An entire family has woken up with very bad headaches. You arrive at the family's house. It seems pretty normal inside, although it is a bit stuffy. It has been one of the first really cold days of fall. Many people are running their furnaces for the first time this season.

The owner of the house is talking to one of your crew. His face is really red. He tells the paramedic he has a bad headache. He also says that his wife and two children have headaches. Something doesn't seem right. What do you think is going on?

A severe headache can be a sign of carbon monoxide poisoning.

More than a Headache

When a furnace gets dirty or does not work properly, it can give off carbon monoxide. If these harmful fumes build up inside a house, they make people sick. Sometimes these fumes can be deadly. This illness is called carbon monoxide poisoning.

Paramedics know that headaches and red cheeks can be a sign of carbon monoxide poisoning. In this case, harmful fumes in the house were making the family sick.

Treatment for Carbon Monoxide Poisoning

- Get the victims out of the house or other enclosed area and into the fresh air.
- Give them oxygen to help them breathe.
- Take them to the nearest hospital.

carbon monoxide: a poisonous gas given off when fuel is burned
fume: a gas, smoke, or vapor

Dog on Ice

It's winter, and a call comes in to help a dog that is trapped on an island of ice. A warm spell has caused the ice on a frozen lake to break apart. The dog is floating on a piece of ice, surrounded by frigid water.

You arrive at the scene. The dog's owner and a few other people have gathered near the shoreline. You put on a wet suit, secure a rope to yourself, and crawl out on the ice. If the ice breaks and you fall into the water, the wet suit will keep you warm and dry. Your partner can pull you to safety with the rope.

Luckily, you do not fall in. You lasso the dog's body with a rescue rope and pull him to safety.

You saved the dog, but that wasn't your only job on this call. This was also an emergency for humans. Can you guess why?

---

frigid: very cold
wet suit: a close-fitting suit made of rubber used to keep the body warm in cold water
secure: to fasten or fix in a firm way
lasso: to loop a rope over an animal's head or body to catch it

Protecting People, Too

There was a danger that others at the scene would try to rescue the dog. People weigh more than dogs and could break through the ice. If someone fell into the ice-cold water, they could only stay alive a very short time.

You and the paramedics were not only there to save the dog. You were also there to keep people off the ice and to help in case a person needed to be saved.

Paramedics practice a rescue in icy water.

A Hot Emergency

This time it's summer. A woman watching a road race sees a runner collapse on the street. She calls 9-1-1. The call comes in to the station and you drive to the race site.

When you arrive, you find the ill runner sitting up in the shade. He does not feel well. He says he feels dizzy and has a bad headache.

Your partner examines the runner. His skin is hot and very dry. What is his problem? What should you do to help?

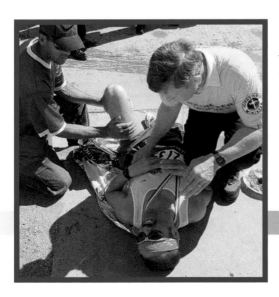

A paramedic assists a runner who has collapsed in the heat.

examine: to check over carefully

Keeping Your Cool

This runner has signs of heatstroke. Heatstroke happens when the body overheats and can't cool itself back down by sweating. The signs of heatstroke are nausea, headache, dizziness, and muscle cramps. Here are some ways paramedics treat heatstroke.

Treatment for Heatstroke

- Get the person indoors, where it is cooler.
- Put damp cloths against the person's skin and run fans to cool down the body.
- Put ice packs under the person's arms and against the groin.
- Keep the person lying down, with the feet slightly higher than the head.
- Use an IV to provide fluids to the person.

groin: the area where the top of the legs joins the upper body
IV: short for *intravenous*; a way to place fluids directly into a vein in the body

Where Do You Look?

A man finds his neighbor confused, drowsy, and breathing very fast. She seems very ill. The man calls 9-1-1.

You arrive and talk to the woman. She cannot say what is wrong. Her eyelids flutter and then stay closed. She falls unconscious right in front of your eyes!

You need to know what is happening to her. Is she taking any medicine? Does she have any health problems? How would you find this kind of information if the woman can't answer your questions?

This new medical alert watch can provide a paramedic with important information about the wearer at the touch of a button in case of an emergency.

---

drowsy: sleepy
flutter: to open and close quickly
unconscious: not able to feel and think; not aware

Hunting for Clues

There are many ways paramedics learn about a patient's health. Here are a few:

When Your Patient Can't Talk

- Look for medicine bottles in the kitchen, bedroom, bathroom, purse, or pockets to see if the patient is taking medication.

- See if the patient is wearing a medical information bracelet that describes any health problems.

- Look on the refrigerator or find an address book for a doctor's phone number and call it.

- Talk to people who know the patient.

- Search for clues with your eyes, nose, and ears.

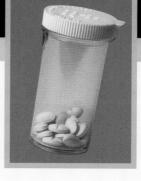

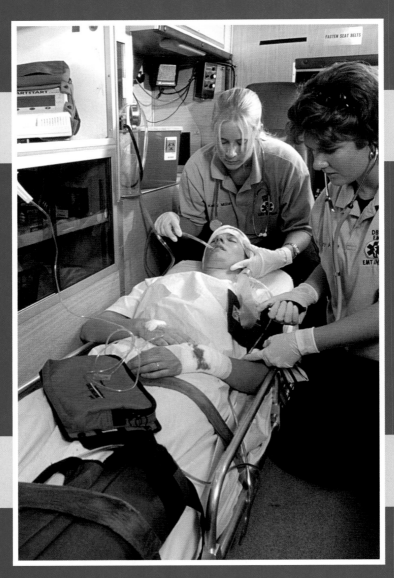

It takes teamwork to safely treat and transport a patient.

Always Alert

Paramedics must be alert and curious, and they must pay close attention to small things when they go out on a call. They often have to act like medical detectives— looking for hidden clues to help someone. This kind of alertness has saved many lives.

How did you do on your calls? Were you able to guess what was wrong with these patients? Are you beginning to think like a paramedic? Do you think you have what it takes to be one?

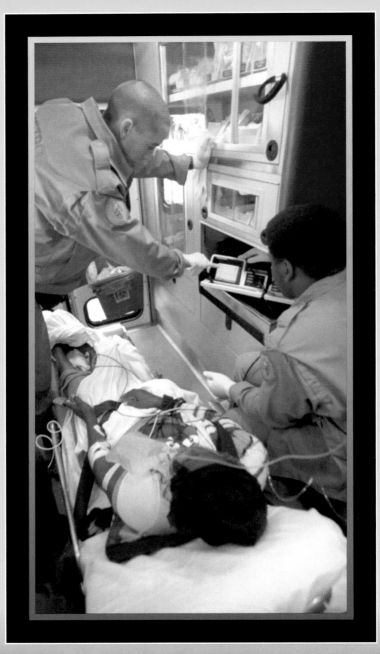

No two days are alike in the life of a paramedic.

CHAPTER 5

Do You Have What It Takes?

WANTED

Men and women to work as a team to save lives. You must care about people, think quickly, and solve problems. You must also be physically fit. We will train you in lifesaving skills. Be ready to learn and keep learning every day.

The Big Picture

A typical paramedic's day can start with an automobile accident and end with a heart attack. In between, you may deliver a baby, give an antidote to a poison victim, and dress the wounds of a burn victim. Being a paramedic is an exciting job. Often it is rewarding. But sometimes, it is stressful. Does this sound like a job for you?

---

antidote: medicine taken to act against a poison
dress: to put medicine and bandages on a wound

Four Levels of Paramedics

Becoming a paramedic requires training. How much training depends on the type of paramedic you want to be. While it varies by state, there are generally four levels of paramedics.

First Responders

First Responders provide basic care or first aid to patients. They are the people who are the first to arrive at the scene. Many police officers and firefighters have this most basic level of training.

EMT-Basic (EMT-1s)

EMT stands for "Emergency Medical Technician." These men and women provide the first level of emergency care. They are trained to assess a patient's condition and treat breathing, heart, and trauma emergencies. They also transport victims to the hospital.

---

assess: to find out
trauma: a bodily injury or wound

EMT-Intermediate (EMT-2s or 3s)

The next level of EMT requires more advanced training. As with EMT-1s, this level can use defibrillators (dee-FIB-rah-LAY-ters) to give shocks to a stopped heart. In addition, EMT-2s or 3s can use other advanced tools to help a person who is not breathing properly. They can also give intravenous (in-trah-VEE-nus) fluids.

EMT-Paramedic (EMT-4s)

This is the highest level of EMT training. These paramedics can do all the duties of the other EMTs. In addition, they may give oral and intravenous drugs, and use more complex equipment to monitor and perform emergency procedures.

---

defibrillator: a tool that provides an electric shock to start or stabilize a patient's heart
complex: not simple; difficult to use or understand
procedure: a way or method of doing something

Getting Started

As a future paramedic, your training begins in a classroom. There you will learn about the human body. You will use that knowledge to learn to recognize a patient's illness or injury. You will be taught to assess what emergency care is required. You will be trained to use a number of lifesaving medical tools. You will also learn how to lift, move, handle, and transport patients as part of pre-hospital emergency care.

Paramedics must be able to get to emergencies quickly and safely. You will learn how to safely handle emergency rescue vehicles. You also will learn how to use heavy rescue equipment to free people trapped in cars, buildings, or other structures. You will be trained how to properly use radios and telephones to communicate with other members of an emergency team.

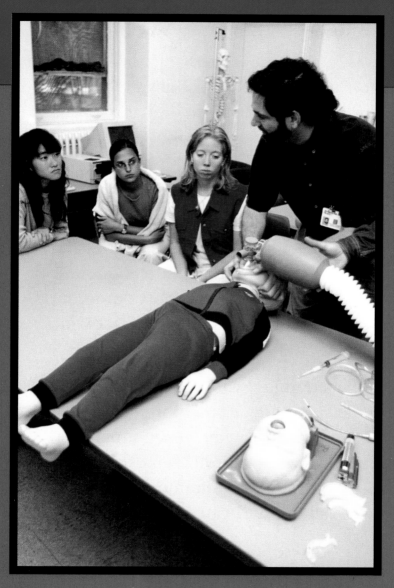

A paramedic's career starts in the classroom.

In the Emergency Room

Your paramedic training next will focus on how to learn lifesaving skills by watching. For this, you will observe what happens in the hospital emergency room.

During this training, you will spend several weeks or months seeing how doctors and nurses work with patients. You will see how lifesaving tools and techniques are properly used. You will learn about and perform advanced life-support procedures. You will also learn how to interact with patients and the medical staff.

This training will help you better understand how to care for people when responding to an emergency situation. You also will learn teamwork skills to help you better communicate and work with other health-care workers.

---

interact: to communicate; to work with others

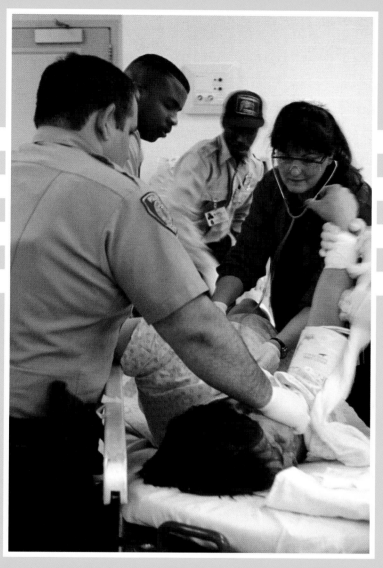

Paramedics work with doctors and nurses in a hospital emergency room.

In the Field

Your third part of paramedic training will be to go out on calls. During this time, skilled paramedics will watch and help as you perform a paramedic's job. Here you will apply and practice all that you learned in the classroom and observed at the hospital.

Paramedic students work in the field as part of their training.

Test Time

After your training ends, you will take a state and maybe a national test. When you pass, you can get a license to become a paramedic!

Do You Have the Right Stuff?

We never know when a medical emergency may happen. But it is good to know that skilled and caring people are ready to answer the call—whenever it comes—and to get there in a matter of minutes.

Paramedics are highly trained professionals who are dedicated to helping people. Their work is important and rewarding. But it takes a caring person who is willing to study and work hard to be capable of saving lives. Could you be one of these people?

---

license: a document giving permission for you to do something or own something

Epilogue

Important Breakthroughs

The success of paramedic programs in the 1960s and 1970s was due in large part to the medical training paramedics received. Two other important breakthroughs also helped to make this success possible.

One was a lifesaving technique called cardiopulmonary resuscitation (CAR-dee-oh-PUHL-mah-nair-ee re-SES-ah-TAY-shun) or CPR. CPR was invented in the late 1950s. It is a way of keeping a patient's blood flowing when the heart has stopped. A person presses the patient's chest and blows air into the lungs during CPR.

Another breakthrough was the invention of the defibrillator in 1960. Paramedics have been trained to use this tool to assist heart attack victims. This has saved many lives.

---

breakthrough: a very important discovery
technique: a special way of doing something

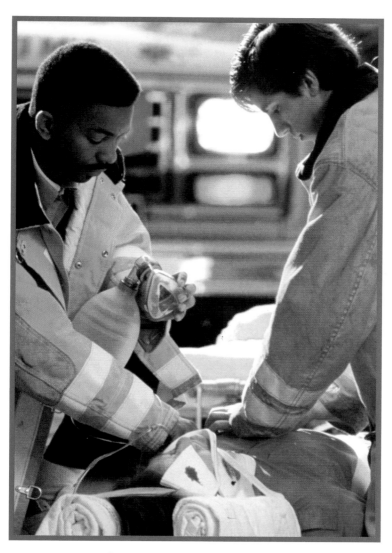

Paramedics give CPR to a heart attack victim.

Glossary

air: to show, tell, or broadcast

ambulance: a special vehicle for carrying injured or sick people

antidote: medicine taken to act against a poison

antivenin: medicine used to prevent poisoning from a snakebite

assess: to find out

aviation: the science, skill, or work of flying airplanes

breakthrough: a very important discovery

carbon monoxide: a poisonous gas given off when fuel is burned

cervical: relating to a neck

complex: not simple; difficult to use or understand

conscious: thought about; considered

crucial: the most important

defibrillator: a tool that provides an electric shock to start or stabilize a patient's heart

dispatcher: a person who receives emergency calls and sends out emergency workers

dress: to put medicine and bandages on a wound

drowsy: sleepy

elite: thought to be the finest or best

emergency: an event that develops suddenly and calls for action right away

EMS: Emergency Medical Service

examine: to check over carefully

flutter: to open and close quickly

focus: to pay close attention to something

forehead: the part of the face above the eyes

frigid: very cold

fume: a gas, smoke, or vapor

groin: the area where the top of the legs joins the upper body

ground: to keep from flying

immobilize: to keep from moving

interact: to communicate; to work with others

IV: short for *intravenous*; a way to place fluids directly into a vein in the body

lasso: to loop a rope over an animal's head or body to catch it

license: a document giving permission for you to do something or own something

medical history: information about a person's past injuries, illnesses, and medicines taken

monitor: to closely watch

oxygen: the gas we need to breathe and live

perspiration: sweat

pre-hospital: before arriving at a hospital

procedure: a way or method of doing something

secure: to make free from danger; to fasten or fix in a firm way

spine board: a hard, flat surface a person lies on that keeps the backbone from moving

stable: staying the same; not getting worse

stretcher: a light bed, sometimes on wheels, used to carry injured or sick people

symptom: something that shows you have an illness or injury

technique: a special way of doing something

trauma: a bodily injury or wound

treatment: a course of action

unconscious: not able to feel and think; not aware

undertaker: a person who arranges funerals

venom: the poison of some snakes, spiders, scorpions, and other animals

ventilator: a machine that allows air to pass through to a person's lungs

wet suit: a close-fitting suit made of rubber used to keep the body warm in cold water

winch: to pull up something using a rope wrapped around a drum, which is turned by a crank or motor

Bibliography

Bryan, Nichol. *Paramedics*. Everyday Heroes. Edina, Minn.: Abdo Publishing, 2003.

Cooney, Caroline B. *Emergency Room*. New York: Scholastic Books, 1994.

Gibson, Karen Bush. *Emergency Medical Technicians*. Mankato, Minn.: Bridgestone Books, 2001.

Masoff, Joy. *Emergency!* Community Helpers. New York: Scholastic Books, 1999.

Useful Addresses

American Red Cross
Chapter Headquarters
2131 K Street, N.W.
Washington, D.C. 20037

National Highway Transportation Safety Foundation
c/o U.S. Department of Transportation
400 7th Street S.W.
Washington, D.C. 20590

The National Paramedic Society
PO Box 1400
Clinton, MS 39060-1400

Internet Sites

FEMA for Kids
www.fema.gov/kids

How to Use 911
www.kidshealth.org/kid/watch/er/911.html

U.S. Fire Administration Kids Page
www.usfa.fema.gov/kids

When It's Just You in an Emergency
www.kidshealth.org/kid/watch/er/emergency.html

Index